US NATIONAL
DEBT RECOVERY

A Program Proposal

ELIAS HILL

iUniverse LLC
Bloomington

US NATIONAL DEBT RECOVERY
A PROGRAM PROPOSAL

iUniverse books may be ordered through booksellers or by contacting:

iUniverse
1663 Liberty Drive
Bloomington, IN 47403
www.iuniverse.com
1-800-Authors (1-800-288-4677)

ISBN: 978-1-4759-9233-5 (sc)
ISBN: 978-1-4759-9234-2 (e)

Library of Congress Control Number: 2013909542

Printed in the United States of America.

iUniverse rev. date: 6/27/2013

This is dedicated to all conscientious US citizens and residents who are actively educating themselves concerning our national economic situation and who are taking the steps necessary to live their lives striving for a more solid economic infrastructure in our nation.

Contents

Contents

Introduction

During 1966 to 1989, I worked for the US Department of State as a certified industrial engineer specializing in efficiency. I focused my energy on assessing underdeveloped foreign countries in creating and improving various national endeavors. I was instrumental in conducting detailed assessments that focused on the operational strategies and conditions of various industries abroad. These assessments allowed me to prescribe workable and affordable solutions aimed at achieving greater economic and industrial gains in a timely manner. As part of my duties I was also instrumental in locating and securing reliable investors to support and carry the projects forward. I was successful in implementing national projects in Bolivia, Peru, Guatemala, Paraguay, Honduras, Nicaragua, Costa Rica, El Salvador, and Panama, as well as in other South American countries.

In this proposal I am responding as a concerned US citizen to the urgent need for regaining control of our national economic situation, directly challenging willing

US citizens to accept and recognize this situation. Consider this proposal as a personal invitation for concerned citizens to join forces to create a nonprofit foundation in which they can work together, utilizing the approaches outlined within this proposal, to achieve a deliberate and focused path to national debt reduction.

Background Information

Our country is in need of immediate assistance to recover from the present national debt crisis. As US citizens we must take action to halt and reverse the continued increase of our national debt, for it will inevitably destroy the foundation of our nation.

The best illustration of our economic situation can be seen in real time at www.usdebtclock.org. [1] You be the judge.

For example, on September 30, 2011, at 11:38:56 PM GMT, the outstanding national debt was reported by the US National Debt Clock at $14.79 trillion:

$$\$14,790,340,540,978.12$$

If we look at the clock's real-time figures, we see that they merely reflect the values at a specific point in time. The estimated population of the United States on September 30, 2011, was 311,347,870. Using the estimated population and the $14.79 trillion [2] in debt, we can determine that the amount owed by each US citizen is on average $47,504.00 of our national debt. If we correlate the debt to actual taxpayers, it can then be said that on September 30, 2011, each taxpayer owed approximately $131,517. Let's not forget that those figures are ever changing and are much less than the present-day figures.

These facts can assist us in addressing other related debt issues before this crisis reaches a point of no return. We have already experienced the fall of powerful banks and first-class corporations, which has increased our rates of unemployment and poverty. The overall reaction has created a sense of economic panic that has driven some individuals to act out their fears, leading to demonstrations and acts of violence.

These events are advance warnings of worse things yet to come if we continue neglecting this ever-growing economic debt crisis. Our economic situation will lead us to a state of national anarchy and conflict between the "haves" and "have-nots." The present wrongs in our society were unthinkable in our youth, yet we are witnessing a new and troubled America.

The actual debt in the United States is the sum of all outstanding debts owed by the federal government for each fiscal year (October 1 to September 30). This debt consists of the public debt and all government trust funds. During the 2011 fiscal year, the public debt was $9.854 trillion [3], owed to the people, businesses, and foreign governments that held treasury bills, notes, or bonds. The trust funds were at \$4.936 trillion, owed by the government to itself. These were running surpluses of other accounts that were placed in the common federal pouch, to be used as regular federal expending funds, no longer set aside and tagged for a specific use. Placing these funds into the federal pouch was considered a logical action because those funds were incorporated as a loan at zero interest. Nevertheless, this move has unbalanced the nation's future economic status in general and in particular as it relates to the future of our Social Security system.

Today many individuals feel insecure and oppressed due to the government's growing inability to ensure the future of their Social Security payments. The population most affected by this situation is the baby boomers as they reach retirement age. Most people are convinced that the centralization of Social Security was a mistake in the first place, as it doesn't permit the Social Security Administration to manage and increase its own funds, placing them in what appeared then to be safe interest-bearing accounts.

This is only a small portion of the financial chaos our nation is experiencing as a result of this growing debt. For instance, during the five-year period from 2006 to 2011, the debt increased an average of \$3.49 billion per day [4], with no realistic solution in sight from the government. As you can see, it is urgent for us, the people, to save our nation from this financial catastrophe. A total national bankruptcy would bring severe consequences not just for all Americans, but also for the world at large.

The following is a proposal designed to completely eradicate our public debt in approximately twenty-five years. It is imperative to start this process now.

The Proposal

In order for any financial proposal to be successful, four key components are required:

I. **Program Goals and Objectives:** Focused on an honest and dignified purpose

II. **Project Parameters:** Pertinent considerations of all activities, major issues, and controls

III. **Project Design:** Includes a comprehensive and reliable system of evaluation and feedback

IV. **Organizational Support:** Donors, contributors, and volunteers as the stronghold of the movement, involving varied constituents from our citizenry who will provide solid support for the project

I. Program Goals and Objectives

The goals and objectives for the program are the following:

- liberate our nation from its worst problem: the national debt crisis;
- place our country on a solid financial foundation, free of foreign economic pressures;
- guarantee the financing of all social programs, especially those that provide work incentives and benefits for lower-income populations;
- establish a solid income base with which the government can comply with all of its financial requirements;
- prevent any future financial situations that would lead us to financial ruin.

Accomplishing these goals and objectives will allow us to regain our economic prestige and to preserve our ability not only to help others, as we have been doing, but also to secure a stronger, solid, and more peaceful society in which we all may live with dignity.

II. Project Parameters

Designing a down-to-earth project requires the recognition of issues related to various parameters, activities, and controls dealing with our intricate national financial situation. The following twenty-one issues must be recognized and then addressed:

1. Our national debt has already reached a dangerous level.

2. Government debt-reduction proposals lead to political-party disputes that fail to define dependable corrective measures.

3. Governments require money to pay for the multitude of activities they conduct.

4. High taxes limit investors' power to develop new enterprises and also decrease people's standard of living.

5. Tax reductions directly affect the revenues of the nation.

6. Property taxes provide a major part of the government's income; however, few can agree on a fair system of taxation for retired seniors with fixed incomes.

7. Governments at times engage in fraudulent activities carried out by unscrupulous politicians and private negotiators for their own private gain.

8. Governments keep people uninformed of certain facts to conceal mistakes, engage in corrupt practices, and/or protect secure information.

9. Governments at times use contingency funds for purposes other than those for which they were intended.

10. All economic activities require strict financial policies and clear and open management controls.

11. Recessions are tragic economic events that affect the finances of most, in particular those of the lower-income classes.

12. The housing industry is the leading and most affected business during a recession; if no corrective measures are applied, there will be a negative impact on employment.

13. Overstaffed governments are hard to control,

generate higher expenses, and operate inefficiently. It is therefore inappropriate for governments to overstaff to reduce unemployment.

14. Property taxes have been the main reason for many families losing their homes, which in turn increases the homeless population.

15. In the United States we have a consumer economy; two-thirds of its total production, plus a large amount of imported products, are locally consumed. The buying power of the United States plays an important economic role in many countries, which in turn is key to our foreign policy as it relates to creating stable world employment.

16. Unemployment generates unemployment. First, it reduces consumers' buying power, which reduces consumption, which in turn reduces production demand; reduced demand in turn further increases unemployment.

17. In a capitalistic system like ours, employment depends on the private sector to provide jobs for the entire available workforce. Nevertheless, the private sector lacks that capacity, leaving a certain percentage of the population unemployed. This creates a need for unemployment compensation, reducing revenues and further affecting the national economy.

18. Unemployment percentage is a key indicator of a nation's economic health. In the United States most scholars consider any unemployment above 4 percent to be a cause for concern. Presently, our unemployment percentages are in constant flux; however, at one point in 2012 it was more than twice this figure.

19. Productivity is a key measure of efficiency of

production, which serves to lower costs and improve quality. These are vital factors in motivating consumer spending habits. Yet higher productivity also creates unemployment due to reduced requirements for labor.

20. National debts in other parts of the world are also causing negative results. Some countries with far less debt than ours are nationalizing private enterprises as a last resort to "increase" government revenues. This alternative not only discourages private investment but also affects employment capacity and general development.

21. Most Americans are tired of our present economic situation and are hoping for a better economy that is capable of motivating local private investments and guaranteeing stable employment for our entire workforce.

III. Project Design

This proposal was designed according to the laws of our nation to help us overcome the negative effects of our present economic situation related to our public debt. This endeavor should be registered and operated as a nonpartisan, nonprofit, and benevolent people's organization.

Furthermore, this proposal is based on confidence in the government's ability to facilitate every aspect of a nationwide endeavor to raise the needed funds to reach the established project goals. The project will consist of donation campaigns, lotteries, raffles, arts and entertainment events, games, special sales, and a variety of special events in which people can participate.

At no time will the project provide funds to the government. The project will select what to finance in accordance with its objectives, and it will make arrangements with the government's help to cover all necessary debt. This is not only to enforce the established project control system but also to ensure that no project funds will be used as general government income to be spent as part of the standard federal budget. The project will establish means for compensating people for their time and effort as they assist with all aspects of the proposal.

The proposal plans to free the government of $8 trillion, equivalent to about 51 percent of the total present national debt of $15.789 trillion, of which 75 percent of this total outstanding public debt is $10.737 trillion. As you may recall, the public debt is that owned by individual investors, corporations, states, local governments, and foreign governments, borrowed at an average interest of 3.143 percent.

The project will concentrate on paying, first of all, foreign debts, at about $4.734 trillion, where the main debt owners are the following: [5]

- China at $1.22 trillion
- Japan at $912 billion

- The United Kingdom at $347 billion
- Taiwan at $153 billion
- Hong Kong at $122 billion

The remaining $1.98 trillion is owed to several other foreign countries.

Project Plan

1. The project plan is to pay the $8 trillion of the public debt in two stages. The first stage consists of a refinancing period during which the project gathers a reasonable amount of funds to start refinancing government debts at half the interest rate the government is currently paying. In other words, the government will continue owing the same amount, to this project, but at a much lower interest rate.

2. The second stage consists of motivating the government to operate at zero deficits, without incurring any additional debt. As soon as the project is in possession of $4 trillion (half of the total program amount), it will go into the actual debt liberation stage. This stage consists of liberating 10 percent of the total debt amount in the project's account at the completion of the first five years during which the government operates with no deficit.

3. At the same time, the project will continue raising funds and refinancing government debts at half the interest rate until it reaches the actual total target amount of $8 trillion.

4. The project will liberate 25 percent of the total government's debt remaining in the project's account when the government has successfully operated for ten years without a deficit.

5. The project will liberate 50 percent of the total government debt remaining in the project's account when the government has successfully operated for fifteen years in the black.

6. The project will liberate 100 percent of the total government debt remaining in the project's account when the government has successfully operated for twenty years with no deficit.

   In the event the government, for any reason, fails to meet the required incentive conditions to qualify for the established benefits, the incentive will go back to the 10 percent level no matter at what level it was already earning; at any time the government fails to complete a single year at no deficit and no additional debt, the project will start counting from that date the five years needed to earn the beginning incentive of 10 percent.

7. The committees will submit clear monthly reports to the project's top management and at each corresponding feedback point within the control system. These reports, in addition to relevant findings, must include a simple assessment of how the payment of the federal debt is affecting the economic growth of our nation.

   To comply with this vital task, the project will form and train special committees to monitor each of these activities. Each committee member is to participate as a nongovernment employee without voice in all official discussions and decision-making activities concerning these matters. Furthermore, the government is expected to provide the project's staff with the required permits and meet conditions of monitoring all actions.

The government will have no difficulty in paying the other $2.737 trillion of the public debt, which the project is not intended to cover. The government can pay the difference by dedicating only a portion of the interest savings generated by the project. Once the government is totally free of the public debt, then and only then will it be in an excellent position to comply with the obligations of the (approximately $5 trillion) no-interest debt.

In short, through this proposal the people of the United States are granting the government the incredible opportunity of liberating itself of payments of $28 billion per month in interest alone through the elimination of over $10.73 trillion of debt at an average interest rate of 3.143 percent.

In essence, to control the time and conditions for granting the established benefits, the project needs to monitor all government activities related to budgeting, spending, borrowing, and debt management concerns.

Banking, accounting, and auditing projects financed with donations and gifts require easy fund-collection routines and very strict controls backed with acid-proof verifications to ensure honest performance.

Banking: The project will establish a solid nationwide banking support structure capable of fulfilling all the project's needs, such as the following:

1. Creating a reliable yet simple deposit system for accepting contributions of any amount
2. Maintaining available deposit records for a verification system in which the project publishes the number and amount of each deposit. Such a system will allow contributors to verify their specific contributions and prevent any discrepancies from occurring. Contributors will be asked to denounce any contributions showing any discrepancies or misallocations by reporting the situation to a special reporting agency.
3. Facilitating the creation and maintenance of sub-accounts to control each moneymaking activity

4. Submitting monthly account reports to the agencies responsible for conducting results-comparison checks to confirm and ensure exactness within the system

Accounting: The project will establish a system of accounting that can fully assure all accounting and auditing activities, such as the following:

1. The project will establish a hard-line accounting system, demanding immediate registration of every financial activity.
2. The project will be accessible by all control functions within the system.
3. The project will contain clear strict rules and regulations, in particular for authorizing or denying fund outlays.
4. The project will be linked to the established control system in every respect.

Auditing: No financial activity is free of mistakes, nor is it safe from individuals committing fraud when controls are sporadic or nonexistent. Consequently, the following measures will be taken:

1. The project will establish a series of auditing controls to detect, eliminate, and correct any fraudulent action in a timely manner.

2. The project will establish a full control structure containing a well-embedded feedback system linked to all auditing activities.

3. The project will establish a power authority to intervene at a moment's notice whenever a discrepancy is detected.

4. The project will conduct regular monthly audits with internal project personnel.

5. The project will contract with outside specialized auditing organizations to conduct quarterly audits.

6. The project will establish an ad hoc inspection and investigation committee composed of important influential persons and/or institutions to oversee the activities of the project. Their findings and observations will be made public.

7. The project will be open to audits at the request of any major private group or organization no more than once a year.

8. The project will welcome any government audits to satisfy any official regulations.

IV. Organizational Support

To reach the noble objective of this "National People's Project," it is essential to have the solid support and firm assistance of an ample majority of our society's members and organizations. This is especially so because this proposal's objective directly deals with the government's responsibility for paying the national debt, and also because the people, through this project, want to place our government in a solid position to provide all necessary infrastructures and services our people need to live and function with dignity.

Consequently, this project must obtain the full support of a variety of contributors and volunteers, including the following:

Citizens with a strong financial base are essential to this project; they can supply important economic support, in particular at the beginning. American members of the Forbes 400 list are the richest American leaders, who on the whole influence the shape of our economy. As concerned philanthropists they are capable of private initiatives created for the public good and that focus on improving the quality of life of the people. A leader among this group of individuals is therefore invited to join this endeavor and provide the necessary financial, structural, and moral support it needs to achieve its full potential. In times of great need visionaries of high moral quality have joined together, putting their individual interests and concerns aside for a noble cause. It is also hoped that all members of the Forbes 400 will work toward the greater good of reducing and eliminating our national debt crisis. Our founding fathers did much the same when they drafted the Constitution of the United States of America.

For instance, the project requires start-up funds to ensure an aggressive start. A single donor could provide this amount or more, setting a philanthropic example to motivate other donors to follow suit. They will be supporting a new type of heroic altruistic national undertaking, and they will be contributing to the ongoing support for this project.

The communication media's involvement is essential to promote the project's image and objective. The media is capable of creating a feeling of national honor in connection with participation in the payment of our country's debt. As the media reports the news, it serves as an intermediary between the government and the people, helping determine which issues are discussed while keeping the public involved in social issues.

It therefore is important for the media to be part of an ad hoc inspection and investigation committee to obtain firsthand information on the project to support their actions related to the project.

The people in general will provide the basic support required for any endeavor to succeed. As stakeholders the people expect any financial project to take all the necessary precautions to meet the expectations of honorable people for an undertaking before they are convinced to support such an endeavor. The noble task of getting rid of our nation's debt requires nothing less. The project will create a system of accountability above everything else to provide clear information concerning the people's contributions and their use toward achieving the established goal. All this must be highlighted by the incentives of honor and patriotism as fighters for our nation's economic stability and progress.

The human resources available in the nation's workforce are its greatest asset. The personnel for such a project must provide qualified, honest management and execution of the enterprise. The administration will go to extremes to secure the best employees and volunteers to manage and carry out the project's many activities and daily tasks.

All activities, including special entertainment projects, will be carried out by qualified honest individuals and groups who volunteer their services, time, and expertise for the sole purpose of raising funds to reach the objective. The project will establish special committees to assist these groups in all their activities, as well as to block any actions that do not comply with the moral standards and decorum required by the proposal.

The people's representatives in our government, as individuals and as citizens, must play an important role in reaching the project's goal. The project will do everything in its power to obtain the support of the people's representatives of all parties, with the full understanding that it will not support any particular political platform, campaign, or activity. Therefore, the project will conduct all its activities in a nonpartisan manner. Any person within the project who violates these guidelines will not be allowed to participate further. It is recommended that all government representatives and political organizations fulfill their duties and obligations in an honest, respectful, and just manner, never taking advantage of their position for self-aggrandizement or to do immoral acts.

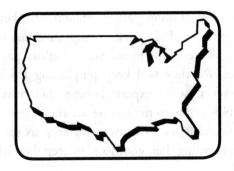

Additional Background Information

Summary of Debt Crisis Data Reviewed for this Proposal

In practice there is nothing wrong with borrowing money to achieve a greater good, provided the debt can be paid back without creating any national adversity. Furthermore, in practice the reverse is also true, and borrowing funds after a point where repayment is impossible is considered irresponsible and an act of cruelty against the people in general, and especially against those who live at or below the poverty level.

Our country for over two centuries managed to borrow money with dignity to finance diverse state affairs, and it fulfilled its financial obligations. In 1917 the United States earned the highest Moody's AAA payback confidence level rating. Yet by August 2011, for the first time, the federal government's credit rating was downgraded from AAA to AA+ [6]. Several US Treasury officials from both parties criticized this new rating as too low, while other financial experts felt the ranking perhaps should have been much lower. Regardless of the rank, foreign investors must still expect the US economy to recover enough to pay back its obligations, for they still keep purchasing US Treasury bills. However, some experts believe their investing in Treasury bills is due to the fact we are the largest customer for their products, and they want to keep us spending to continue importing their goods and to keep their labor force employed.

There is another more popular way of grading a nation's debt. This method evaluates the size of a debt in relation to a GDP percentage. GDP stands for gross domestic product; that is, the value of the total production of a nation during a specific time (usually a year). Most economists give great significance to this percentage. A country with debts of 80 percent or higher of its GDP has fallen into a dangerous payback-reliability zone. The existence of this condition indicates internal economic difficulties, such as lack of credit trust, reduced investment potential, unemployment, increased subsistence demands, and restriction of other social and economic aspects that invite an economic depression. During 2011 the US debt's percentage of GDP was already higher than 100 percent [7]. This figure confirms the belief of those economists that the United States merited a lower Moody's credit rating.

The debt to GDP relation is a variable figure that shows ups and downs through time; the United States is no exception. For instance, from 1960 to 2002 the percentage ranged from 33.4 to 59 percent. Then from 2003 to 2008 the percent ranged from 61.8 to 69.6 percent. Then in 2009 the percentage escalated to 84.4 percent, the highest in forty years. Even higher figures were to come. In 2010 the figure was 93.4 percent, and in 2011 it was slightly above 100 percent [8].

This apparently simple percentage relation often confuses noneconomists because of the two parts of our national debt: the public debt, which reflects only the interest-demanding debt, not giving much significance to the trust fund obligations (an internal debt within the government in itself that is free of interest). On the other hand, most consider the total of the two parts of our national debt to be more realistic because sooner or later the government has to come up with the funds needed to cover those obligations. These different concepts yield different scenarios. For instance, the GDP for 2010 was $14.7 trillion; based on that figure, our total debt was 93.4 percent of GDP, and it was only 62.2 percent if we consider only the public debt [9].

Regardless of the debt-measuring method used, our national debt will continue to increase at an alarming rate unless we all unite and do something pragmatic to save our country from serious economic decay.

To better understand the nature of our present debt, it is important to go a bit into our past. Historically speaking, borrowing is nothing new to the United States. On January 1, 1791, our country, under the Articles of Confederation, had a debt amounting $75.463 million [10]. These funds were used to cover expenses for the American Revolution. From 1791 to 1811 the United States had fourteen years of budget surpluses, allowing for the payment of almost all its debt. Then from 1812 to 1814, as a result of the War of 1812, the debt sharply increased. However, during the following two decades, eighteen years with surpluses allowed the United States to pay off almost all of its debt by the year 1834 [11].

For the next twenty-six years, the United States operated at tolerable levels of debt. In 1860 the debt was $65 million, but as the result of the devastating Civil War, the debt increased, rising for the first time to $1 billion in 1863, and it did not stop there. By the end of the war, in 1865, it had reached $2.7 billion. During the following thirty-five years, the United States closed most fiscal years with surpluses, which allowed for a 55 percent reduction in the debt, leaving the debt total at $1.215 billion by the year 1900

The US Congress is the only branch of the government with the power to borrow money; this authority is granted under Article I, Section 8, of the Constitution. From the founding of our nation until 1917, Congress authorized each individual debt issuance separately. However, in order to provide more flexibility to finance the United States' involvement in World War I, Congress modified the method by authorizing the Liberty Bond Act of 1917 [12]. Under this act, Congress also established a limit, or "ceiling," on the total amount of bonds that could be issued. Liberty war bonds were sold in the United States to support the Allied cause in World War I. Subscribing to bonds became a symbol of patriotism. As expected, the war's high expenses resulted in a major increase; the debt went from $2.912 billion in 1914 to $27.39 billion by 1919. This critical period was followed by ten consecutive years of surpluses, reducing the debt to $16.93 billion by 1929; this was an equivalent reduction of 38.19 percent.

A new era of debt increases started to cover the social programs enacted to get out of the Great Depression. By 1934 the national debt had increased to $27.053 billion, and by 1936 it had increased to $33.7 billion. Increases did not stop here; another debt increase occurred as we set out to finance the US involvement in World War II and to sponsor the European Recovery Program (established to help in the reconstruction of European countries devastated by the war, including enemy nations such as Germany). Our debt increased from 1936 to 1950 to a total of $260 billion. By

1955 the Korean War expenses had brought the total debt to $274.374 billion.

For the next decade (1955–65) the debt increased an average of $4.29 billion per year, reaching a total of $317.273 billion in 1965. For the following decade (1965–75) the debt increased an average of $21.59 billion per year, reaching a total of $533.189 billion by 1975. During this same decade we also added expenses from the Vietnam War.

The following decade (1975–85) was a critical economic period; the debt grew an average of $127 billion per year, reaching a total of $1.823 trillion by 1985. The huge figure of $1 trillion was reached for the first time during early 1982. It was obvious the national debt was in a pattern of increases; however, there still appeared to be a great possibility for recovery. Unfortunately, the government irresponsibly neglected the dangerous position the national debt was placing us in.

During the next decade (1985–95), the debt increased an average of $315.09 billion per year, reaching a total of $4.974 trillion by 1995. This incredibly high yearly increase demonstrates the incapacity, or the lack of desire, of our government to reduce the amount of debt. It was obvious they were supporting the impressive uncontrolled spending pattern to benefit certain groups or individuals. The fact is they were disregarding the people's and the nation's welfare overall. During this time we also fought the first war with Iraq, Operation Desert Storm, which was used to justify the increasing expenditures while ignoring the importance of decreasing the national debt.

For the next five years, from 1995 to 2000, the debt increased an average of $110.4 billion per year, reaching a total of $5.526 trillion by the year 2000. During this period the yearly average increase showed a reduction in comparison to increases in previous years. As far as the debt is concerned, however, there was no improvement, because the debt still increased by $552 billion during that time period.

For the years 2000 to 2005, the debt increased an average of $481.4 billion per year, reaching a total of $7.933 trillion by 2005. This exorbitant increase to the national debt eliminated all credibility of our government's promises to reduce the debt. The pretext for the high expenses was and still is the war against terrorism, which started on September 11, 2001. But in reality, this reason is no longer valid, and it never was as it relates to the exorbitant amount expended on this account. There were a number of opportunities that would have permitted us to avoid such expenditures. However, our leaders neglected those opportunities and insisted on sacrificing more of our brave soldiers while incurring unnecessary expenses and authorizing extended stays of troops abroad.

From 2005 to 2011, the debt increased an average of $1.14 trillion per year, equivalent to $3.17 billion per day, reaching the incredible total of $14.79 trillion by 2011 [13]. In all honesty, this is a "spooky reality." No one can deny the national debt has reached a frightening level and is already generating serious problems. Our nation is crying out, loud and clear, for help through the many situations occurring in our social and political arenas.

Presently, we have a clear understanding of the continual increase in our national debt, but to better understand the whole picture it is necessary to touch on certain topics related to the national debt:

- the debt ceiling
- the budget
- federal spending

Debt Ceiling

As was mentioned previously, Congress is the only branch of government with the official authority to borrow funds; as a result, Congress has the actual authority to set the debt ceiling. This authority has a number of weaknesses, making it possible to overlook certain circumstances in dealing with the need to raise the debt ceiling due to special circumstances. Congress has the authority to set the debt ceiling, but not the authority to control the various elements that create the need to raise the debt limit. Seen another way, it is clear that Congress doesn't have the appropriate legislation to enforce the required provisions to lower the debt.

For instance, some aspects of the process for setting the debt ceiling at times confuse matters. Establishing the debt limit is a separate action from the regular process of financing government operations; as a result, the debt ceiling has no direct impact on preventing budget deficits. The executive branch is obligated to prepare a yearly budget and submit it to Congress for approval; this budget must detail all projected outlays, as well as all expected revenue collections.

When a budget deficit occurs, the government must obtain the extra needed funds during the same fiscal year, which requires increasing the debt ceiling. Congress must first approve such an increase, but if Congress delays the required approval, the country enters into what is known as a "debt ceiling crisis." Such a crisis occurred in mid-2011 when the two houses of Congress were unable to agree on a revision in the proposed debt ceiling [14].

This crisis was resolved though one of the legalities of the system. A debt-ceiling-increase authorization may be applied in a variety of ways. When the debt ceiling is reached, the treasury can declare a debt issuance suspension period and utilize "extraordinary measures" to acquire funds to meet federal obligations while not requiring a new debt. The treasury first used this measure on December 16, 2009, to remain within the debt ceiling and avoid a government shutdown; it was used again during this last crisis in 2011 [15]. However, there are limits to how much the debt ceiling can be raised by this method.

There have been other attempts to facilitate increases in the debt ceiling. In 1979 the House of Representatives passed a rule to automatically raise the debt ceiling when a budget is passed, eliminating the need for a separate vote on the debt ceiling—except when the House votes to waive, or repeal, this rule. The exception to this rule was invoked in 1995, but again, the lack of agreement resulted in a government shutdown.

The debt ceiling authorization is an exercise full of complexities with no solid practical authority. It is further complicated by bizarre political behavior in both houses of Congress every time they have to authorize a debt ceiling change. This shameful political behavior is the product of the constant irrational political rivalry between Republicans and Democrats. Not in vain, the Government Accountability Office (GAO) explains, "The debt limit does not control or limit the ability of the federal government to run deficits or incur obligations. Rather, it is a limit on the ability to pay obligations already incurred" [16].

The apparent irrelevancy of the debt ceiling has led many to suggest it should be abolished altogether. The problems that occur in authorizing a debt ceiling increase relate to one party attempting to gain political advantage over the other.

Budget

The federal budget involves an intricate and complex process. The president submits a proposed budget to Congress on the first Monday in February of each year. This budget outlines the strategies and policies he is proposing for that specific fiscal year. The Council of Economic Advisors assists the president by keeping him up to date through the *Economic Report of the President*. In this report they provide him with a thorough analysis of the upcoming economic trends.

The actual groundwork for preparing the budget is carried out by the executive Office of Management and Budget (OMB). They are in charge of preparing the budget for the president for submission to Congress. This office also manages the budget throughout the year, working with the Congressional Budget Office (CBO), which provides information to Congress to facilitate the budget's review.

Federal Spending

Federal spending is divided into three categories: discretionary, mandatory, and military spending. Each is treated independently, with its own rules and regulations.

- **Discretionary spending** is the part of the federal budget that deals with the thirteen appropriations bills; it is negotiated between the houses of Congress and the president's office each year as part of the budget process. This spending includes everything the federal government requires to operate, including the defense section, which is composed of the Pentagon and its standard programs. This part alone takes a good portion of the discretionary spending. For the fiscal year 2012 the budget proposed discretionary spending at $868 billion, corresponding to 23.5 percent of the total budget [17].

- **Mandatory spending** is for programs required by law to provide certain benefits. For example, for the fiscal year 2012 the budget allotted $2.109 trillion for this spending, which was equivalent to 57 percent of the total budget. These totals included outlays for Social Security at $761 billion, Medicare at $468 billion, Medicaid at $269 billion, the Troubled Asset Relief Program (TARP) at $13 billion, and $598 billion for other government programs such as food stamps, unemployment compensation, child nutrition, tax credits, and supplemental security income for the disabled and for students. Over half the budget (57 percent, as was mentioned above) is dedicated to mandatory programs; the federal government is restricted in discretionary spending. This is one reason why health care reform is often brought to the carpet for consideration [18].

• **Military spending** consists of outlays for programs connected to any war efforts and the active defense of our nation. For the fiscal year 2012 the budget proposed $723 billion (close to $2 billion per day), corresponding to 19.5 percent of the total proposed budget [19].

There is nothing wrong with a federal budget proposal of $3.7 trillion or more, provided the normal revenues are sufficient to pay for all those expenses, plus some extra funds for lowering our overall national debt. Our federal spending is very high in comparison to our normal revenues, however. Year after year, we wind up with deficits and an increased national debt. It is important to note that in order to overpower us, our enemies keep us engaged in wars while encouraging us to spend beyond our present resources. They know they will never defeat us on the front lines, but they also know they can break us down by driving us to a self-induced attrition.

Our national spending is ever increasing and is placing us further out of control. Soon we will reach the state of self-attrition so much desired by our enemies.

Corrective Alternatives: There are three possible alternatives for obtaining the necessary funds to pay for all or part of a debt:

1. Reducing expenses

2. Increasing income
3. Obtaining donations

1. **Reducing expenses** is a good alternative for debt reduction, requiring cutbacks in all superfluous expenses, which are not always a large part of the budget. If necessary, the nation could go into a period of austerity by cutting all expenses to a minimum, while taking special care not to bring any additional hardship to the poor and destitute populations in our society. There are times in our personal lives that we have experienced periods of austerity for different reasons, such as after a natural disaster, a unique setback, a criminal act against us, a medical emergency, and/or an unfortunate accident.

   However, irresponsible government spending has brought our nation into a period of forced austerity like the one we are in now. This situation began prior to the so-called 2008 economic recession; and in spite of our sacrifices, our national debt continues to increase, which can only worsen our personal economic situation as well.

2. **Increasing the income** available is another alternative. In the United States, capitalism as an economic system creates serious limitations that do not permit us to enter into business ventures to obtain additional funds. Practically the only alternative available for the federal government is to raise taxes. This is easily said, but it is full of complications. The poor cannot be part of this process, and the middle class

is rapidly losing economic stability due to the rising costs of necessities. The wealthy also want to avoid higher taxes, and we are better served by their role in providing job opportunities for the general population, thus boosting economic growth. Raising taxes for these individuals would affect their ability to continue to bring about growth in the job market. If jobs cease to exist, this would be very detrimental to the nation's economic well-being; thus, the debates continue among our leaders today.

Hypothetically, the problem this alludes to is as follows: If businesses no longer can generate the necessary jobs to hire the total workforce, the number of taxpayers decreases; this affects the amount of taxable income, and this in turn creates other expenses related to unemployment. On the other hand, if the government cannot raise taxes to gather the required funds to pay for the nation's expenses, the result will be to go further into debt in spite of the consequences.

3. **Obtaining donations** is a standard method used by nonprofit (tax-free) organizations that help others deal with specific needs or problems. But by all means, we cannot expect our national government to start a fundraising campaign for any specific budget item. The government has the power to obtain funds through taxes, which is the normal legal established method for obtaining additional funds. But as was mentioned previously, raising taxes is seriously

restricted in relation to the amounts and from whom they are collected.

Large National Debts

The US national debt is indeed the largest in the whole world, but it is not the only one that is out of control. As a matter of fact, several countries presently are facing worse economic conditions as a result of their national debt. It is not wise for us to minimize the importance of our debt crisis just because others are facing worse conditions than we are. We should take the leading role in solving our problem and set an example for other nations to follow.

This proposal has taken into consideration the difficulties other nations around the world are experiencing as a result of their large national debts. Our fellow humans' successes and failures have served as vivid examples for us in designing this proposal.

The European Union is in the midst of a possible disintegration because of uncontrollably large debts in some of its member nations. Leading the pack and sinking deep into this financial chaos are Greece, Spain, Italy, Ireland, and Portugal. The people in those nations are voicing their dissatisfaction though uncontrollable demonstrations against the rich and powerful; this is affecting the stability and peace of many European nations as many key government officials have been forced to resign.

Let's take a depressing example: Greece, a small country in the Mediterranean Sea, has been surviving since May 2010 on a first bailout of €110 billion ($147 billion) [20]. Their financial crisis was so severe that a second rescue was soon needed, as the country remained locked out of the international bond markets by its sky-high interest rates and the instability of its unsustainable national debt. During a European marathon negotiation, it was agreed to give Greece another bailout loan of €130 billion ($179 billion), including a rescue loan and bank support allowing banks to write off 50 percent of the Greek debt for €100 billion ($138 billion). This occurred under what is termed a "credit default swap," in which lenders lose the swapped amount. This measure no doubt benefits Greece, but it leaves the European financial crisis in a bigger predicament.

On the whole, the European financial crisis has reached a dangerous level, to the point that the finance ministers of the seventeen countries under the euro project are doing everything possible not only to save their currency but also to prevent a European Union breakdown. They are trying to find the means to fully integrate the dissimilar euro-zone nations (politically, financially, and culturally), including every nation—from powerful Germany to tiny Malta. They already know from experience that they must act quickly and avoid imposing any ineffective measures as they have in the past, resulting in many unstable European reforms.

They fear this crisis, which already has forced the bailouts of Greece, Ireland, Portugal, and Spain, and could swallow up bigger economies. In order to lessen the European financial crisis, most members of the European Union, motivated by Germany and France, got together and agreed on a stronger "European Financial Union," establishing a budgetary disciplinary regime with automatic sanctions to those nations that don't follow the rules. Among other agreements, Europe is to strengthen the International Monetary Fund with €200 billion to provide loans to European nations with temporary financial problems. This arrangement was to take effect in July 2012 [21]. The world of finance hoped the best would result from this agreement causing a positive impact on the stock market. However, the very next day the stock market complained loudly as a result of the Fitch Ratings analysis of the situation. In effect, the European debt crisis continues to be unresolved.

Nevertheless, many poor countries with limited incomes depend on donations from other countries or international organizations to fulfill their most pressing needs. We, as citizens of the United States, will never allow our country to resort to those approaches. We are proud citizens and can create the necessary means to pull our country out of any crisis when we set our minds and hearts to do it; this proposal is designed to do just that. It is time for the rich and powerful to proceed on behalf of the less privileged through a solid national recovery program that guarantees gainful employment for everyone willing to engage in honest work.

We have much to learn, both positive and negative, from small nations such as Greece, for their national debt has caused them and the world in general so much grief in spite of the many efforts they have made to reduce their increasing debt. However, these problems are nothing in comparison to what Europe and the rest of the world would suffer if a larger nation were to fail to fulfill its debt obligations. For instance, imagine the turmoil that would result if Italy were to default on its debt obligations. I selected this country because Italy is the euro zone's third largest, with an uncontrolled debt amounting to €1.9 trillion ($2.5 trillion), and it already is facing increasing debt problems [22]. The fallout could expand not only through the entire euro project but also throughout the global economy; it is already creating panic and affecting stock market decisions.

Picture for a moment the chaos the United States of America would create—not only for itself but for the world at large—if it were to default on its debt obligation. As you can surmise, we owe it to ourselves, to our country, and to all of humanity to do something effective and fast about our national debt crisis. We must stay focused on the simple fact that getting more loans to pay debt owed does not solve anything; on the contrary, it only worsens our financial crisis.

For many years we have been ignoring the clear warning signals of what is to come; if we don't wake up and get out of this financial trap, many unwelcome changes will come our way and affect the basic fiber of our American way of life.

Not long ago it would have been unthinkable for our banks and major corporations to file for bankruptcy as an economic strategy to protect their interests, or for them to ask for direct government assistance. By assisting these businesses, the government increased the national debt and brought about other economic consequences to the general public.

In recent history American Airlines was seeking chapter 11 bankruptcy protection in an effort to deal with their out-of-control debt, which resulted from inappropriate management practices [23]. They justified their economic situation by blaming the high cost of jet fuel and labor struggles. Other airlines faced similar situations with the cost of fuel and did not resort to such a plan just to continue in operation.

The filing of chapter 11 is a no-win situation for all involved. A large portion of all outstanding debts owed to suppliers and providers of services are never paid. This, in turn, creates a domino effect in which the affected businesses increase their prices in order to recoup their losses. These practices in the end pass the high cost of goods to the people, who are now forced to pay more for basic needs, such as food, gas, and shelter. The public is now affected not only financially but also emotionally and psychologically, as a state of frustration and dismay develops; an unstable social system results.

As businesses continue to raise the price of goods and services to maintain high incomes for their CEOs and top managers, the general public will become more outraged and less likely to assist in any solution related to national debt reduction.

An example of this occurred in 2011 when dozens of Occupy Wall Street protestors invaded Zuccotti Park in New York City as part of a worldwide movement protesting corporate greed and economic inequality. The demonstrators had broken many park rules and managed to impose their ways, taking over the park and using it for months as their headquarters. They even threatened "Things are going to get much bigger than what anyone can imagine." This protest got worldwide support. In Sydney, Australia, supporters waved signs saying, "You can't eat money." In Tokyo, about two hundred people joined the global protests. In Manila, The Philippines, followers marched to the US embassy expressing support for the demonstrators occupying the park near Wall Street, while condemning "US imperialism" and aggression [24].

Demonstrations against the rich and powerful are becoming more aggressive and more difficult to control. The police are forced to apply stricter practices in their attempts to protect the general public. Demonstrators are not only barricading streets, but they are also blocking traffic by standing or sitting on the street. They have overturned trash containers and hurled bottles, putting everyone in danger. In one case a demonstrator sprayed a deputy inspector with an unknown liquid. Later the man declared online that he was HIV positive and that the officer should seek medical attention.

There is no excuse for such out-of-control demonstrations. Demonstrators irresponsibly believe they are engaging in "democracy in action." It is important to help these individuals out of their economic troubles.

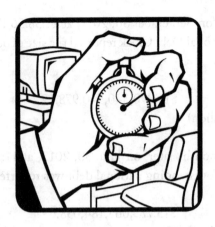

Conclusion

In conclusion, I would like to stress the following:
There is no more time to waste, for our economic turmoil is ever increasing. As Americans we have the obligation to maintain life, liberty, and the pursuit of happiness for ourselves and future generations.

In the United States of America any aggressive group fighting for better economic conditions could easily find many supporters among the economically oppressed. It is imperative we eliminate the possibility of guerrilla warfare on our own land.

It is not easy for many of us to comprehend what a billion dollars is; however, it is practically impossible to get a clear understanding of one thousand billion dollars, or one trillion.

As you may recall, at the start of this proposal it was

stated that on September 30, 2011, at 11:38:56 PM GMT, the US National Debt Clock reported the size of our national debt at

$14,790,340,540,978.12

($14.79 trillion).

Nine months later, on June 30, 2012, at 11:34:56 PM GMT, the outstanding national debt was reported at

$15,789,065,184,058.69

($15.79 trillion) [25].

An increase to the national debt of one trillion dollars in only nine months is not only frightening but also intolerable. We have to accept that the present proposal offers an honorable alternative to liberate our nation from further chaos and economic strife.

Final Comment

I am confident this proposal will have an outstanding response from all Americans, transforming the payment of our national debt into a heroic and dignified act, of which we can all be proud. This achievement, no doubt, will become a powerful example of patriotism for other countries to follow.

We, as patriotic citizens, must respond to this call, concentrating our efforts and intelligence in a united front to eliminate this debt emergency. We still have time to save our nation from the greatest debt crisis it has ever faced.

We can do it together!

Notes

1. US Debt Clock, accessed on September 30, 2011, http://www.usdebtclock.org/.
2. Tom Murse, "Debt Ceiling History. US Government," News & Issues: US Government Info., updated July 12, 2011, http://usgovinfo.about.com/od/federalbudgetprocess/a/US-Debt-Ceiling-History.htm. Accessed February 2012.
3. Tyler Druden, "Zero Hedge," October 3, 2011, http://www.zerohedge.com/news/us-closes-2010-2011-fiscal-year-1479034032855715-debt-95-billion-jump-day-12-trillion-increase.
4. "Historical Debt Outstanding—Annual 2000–2012," Treasury Direct, http://www. treasurydirect.gov/govt/reports/pd/histdebt/histdebt_histo5.htm. Accessed February 2012.
5. "Major Foreign Holders of Treasury Securities," Department of the Treasury/Federal Reserve Board, February 28, 2013, http://www.treasury.gov/resource-center/data-chart-center/tic/Documents/mfh.txt.
6. Don Ayotte, "Standard and Poor downgrades US credit rating from AAA to AA+," Delaware Politics Net, Budget Economy, August 6, 2011, http://www.delawarepolitics.net/category/budget/.
7. Christopher Chantrill, "What is Debt." US Government Spending.com, March 11, 2013, http://www.usgovernmentspending.com/federal_debt_chart.html.
8. Ibid.

9. Ibid.
10. Patt Morrison, "The history of American debt: When did we first borrow, how did it get so out of control?" O89.3 KPCC Southern California Public Radio, July 24, 2011, http://www.scpr.org/programs/patt-morrison/2011/07/25/20022/the-history-of-american-debt-when-did-we-first-bor/.
11. Matt Philips, "The Long Story of the US Debt, from 1790 to 2011 in 1 Little Chart," *The Atlantic*, November 13, 2012, http://www.theatlantic.com/business/archive/2012/11/the-long-story-of-us-debt-from-1790-to-2011-in-1-little-chart/265185/.
12. Ibid.
13. Ibid.
14. Ibid.
15. Ibid.
16. Roanen Barron, commented on Its Our America, "The Fiscal Cliff Debacle," January 7, 2013, http://www.roanen.com/1/post/2013/01/the-fiscal-cliff- debacle.html. Accessed March 11, 2003.
17. The White House, "Fiscal Year 2012 Budget," February 2, 2011, http://www.whitehouse.gov/sites/default/files/omb/budget/fy2012/assets/budget.pdf.
18. Ibid.
19. Ibid.
20. Lefteris Papadimas and Jan Strupczewski, "EU, IMF Agree $147 Billion Bailout for Greece," Athens/Brussels, Reuters, May 2, 2010, http://www.reuters.com/article/2010/05/02/us-eurozone-idUSTRE6400PJ20100502. Accessed August 2012.
21. Mark Koba, "Europe's Economic Crisis: What You Need to Know," CNBC, June 18, 2012, http://www.cnbc.com/id/47689157/Europe039s_Economic_Crisis_What_You_Need_to_Know.
22. "Italy National Debt," Countryeconomy.com, http://countryeconomy.com/national-debt/italy. Accessed August 2012.

23. Gerard J. Arpey and Thomas W. Horton, "AMR and American Airlines File for Chapter 11 Reorganization for Industry Competitiveness," http:// www.aa.com/i18n/ amrcorp/newsroom/fp_restructuring.jsp. Accessed August 2012.

24. Chad Bray, Jessica Firger, Andrew Grossman, and Pervaiz Shallwani, "Judge Rules Against 'Occupy' Protesters," *Wall Street Journal*, November 16, 2011, http://online.wsj.com/ article/SB100014240529702041905045770392536688638 14.html.

25. US Debt Clock, http://www. usdebtclock.org/. Accessed June 30, 2012.

Printed in the United States
By Bookmasters